Veit Etzold

30 Minutes

Effective Change Communication

Bibliographic information from the German National Library
The German National Library lists this publication in the German National Bibliography. Detailed bibliographic information can be found online at http://dnb.d-nb.de.

ISBN 978-3-95623-943-4

Cover design: Martin Zech Design, Bremen
Translation: Hanna Campbell, London
Copyediting: Anja Hilgarth, Herzogenaurach
Author portrait: Pietro Sutera
Typesetting: Zerosoft, Timisoara
Printing: Print on demand, Germany

First published under the title "30 Minuten Wandel kommunizieren" in 2020 by GABAL Verlag, Germany

www.veit-etzold.com

Know more in 30 minutes!

This concise, reliable guide is designed to enable you to get to grips quickly with the topic at hand. A system of signposts guides you through the chapters, allowing you to pick up the basics in slots of 10 to 30 minutes at a time.

A quick, manageable read

The entire book is intended to be readable in just 30 minutes. If you don't have 30 minutes, you can focus on the sections that contain the most relevant information for you.

- **Key information is shown in grey.**
- Key questions with page numbers at the beginning of each chapter allow you to navigate quickly through the book – simply turn to the page you need to bridge existing gaps in your knowledge.
- *Regular content summaries within each chapter facilitate rapid skim-reading…*
- … while a 'Fast Reader' at the end of the book summarizes the most important points.
- Finally, an index at the end of the book enables you to look up particular terms as needed.

Contents

Foreword

Digital transformation, the ascension of new major players (China and others) to the geopolitical stage, millennial-driven changes in consumer behaviour and the increasing demands of shareholders require us and our companies to become continuously better – and thus to find new and different ways of working.

Unfortunately, this challenge is not one that can be met by sticking our heads in the sand and hoping for the best. **Those who do not change proactively will be changed whether they like it or not.** Either we take control and secure a seat at the table, or we end up on the menu.

Against this background, it is not sufficient for you, as a manager, board member or company founder, to merely acknowledge the importance of this cultural shift. Instead, your challenge is to take your employees and other stakeholders with you – because whether you want to drum up enthusiasm for a project, implement a strategy or sell a new product, you must be able to win others over to your goal. **Leadership** is about getting others to strive towards a common objective, ideally with readiness and willingness to do so. Clear communication of the need for change is the best approach to meeting this challenge, and a good story is the best tool at your disposal. Irrespective of what you're trying to achieve, it is vital that you tell a story. Communication cannot occur in a vacuum. If you fail to tell a **positive story about your change project**, others will be quick to swoop in with negative ones: a phenomenon better known as 'speculation and gossip'. This book can help you tell the right story from the outset. It's designed to show how you, as a leader, can communicate change projects unambiguously and with success. This involves:

1. Mapping out a clear change strategy;
2. Developing the right story to communicate your strategy and creating a sense of drama and urgency;
3. Addressing the right stakeholders; and
4. Making creative use of metaphors to illustrate your story.

I wish you plentiful success and enjoyment (yes – both are possible!) with your own programme of transformation and change.

Prof. Dr. Veit Etzold

30 MINUTES

1. Change is a 'necessary evil'

When it comes to the subject of change, leadership coaches and retired managers are fond of propagating a rose-tinted picture: that employees exist in a state of perpetual impatience for the next organizational change. Unfortunately, this is something of a fallacy. **People are creatures of habit**, and so long as their current reality is in some way tolerable, they see no need for major upheaval. The saying 'If it's not broke, don't fix it' is not only one beloved of IT departments around the world. Yet whatever we feel about it, **the fact of the matter is that organizations *must* engage in ongoing change** in order to remain viable. Moreover, such change should not only be triggered as a last resort and fire-fighting measure, since if this is the case, it is probable that any willingness for change will be hindered by a lack of resources to actually achieve it. Equally misguided is the belief that change and transformation were made necessary only by the advent of digitalization. Successful companies and organizations have been evolving constantly for hundreds of years, and successful change has been decisive for their survival.

1.1 Strategy and change

There is an old saying in the consultancy business that 'those who refuse to change will be changed whether they like it or not.' More succinctly: '**Have lunch or be lunch.**' If a company has a pioneering product, it can dominate the market for many years – but if it clings too steadfastly to its previous accomplishments, it may be precisely this antiquated formula for success that leads to its demise. Consider, for example, how French knights' heavy armour – so advantageous in hand-to-hand combat – became an instant liability with the innovation of the crossbow bolt. Whenever a bolt would penetrate the metal plating, the knight would be pinned helplessly to the ground due to the metal's weight.

An uncomfortable world

Thanks to digitalization, the rapid pace of technological advancement, the effects of networking and the emergence of new powers (China and others), the average lifespan of a company is shorter than ever before. Most fail to make it to half the lifespan of the average human (Senge, 1990, p.17). Pentagon strategists speak of a '**VUCA world**': one characterized by **volatility** (fluctuating trends, increasing numbers of crises, 1998, 2001, 2007, 2010 ...), **uncertainty** (Trump, Brexit), **complexity** (global networks) and **ambiguity** (e.g. Facebook, where the 'customer' is also a provider of data, and thus their role is complex and multifaceted).

In a recent interview with the author, Peter Gerber, CEO of Lufthansa Cargo, named what he sees as the **greatest challenges for senior managers** (see https://www.youtube.com/watch?v=6OSjtDNPCjI&t=439s=). These were:

a) the need to set out a coherent strategy;
b) the need to be able to adapt this strategy to a great number of different stakeholders without compromising its coherence; and
c) the need – both before the strategy is implemented, and during it – to be able to make far-reaching decisions on a frequent basis, under high time pressure and without an adequate pool of data.

No-one can deny that we live in uncomfortable times. It is better, then, to effect change of our own volition than to wait for a competitor to serve us up for lunch. Strategy plays a fundamental role in this proactive approach, since it crystallizes the way in which we intend to meet a certain goal.

Strategy as the path to the goal

Strategy lays out the way in which we plan to achieve a goal. If we want to reach the top of a mountain, we can hike there, take a cable car or parachute down onto the summit. Just as with a company strategy, the strategy is based on the opportunities available. The parachute is the quickest method, but is also the most expensive. Hiking up the mountain, on the other hand, is cheap and good for fitness. **A good strategy is not just aligned to the goal, but tailored** to those who wish to achieve it.

Within a strategy, the individual measures that form the path to the goal are the **tactical steps.** In the above example, the first step might be to look for a pair of hiking boots. The second might be to gather equipment; the third might be to set out on the route. In many cases, the individual tactical steps do not immediately reveal the broader strategic goal. If you boarded an aircraft and jumped out of it with a parachute, onlookers would be unlikely to guess that your intention was to reach the summit. In the business world, such ambiguity might usefully be pursued deliberately so as to confuse your competitors about your intentions. Bruce Henderson, founder of the Boston Consulting Group (BCG) and a pioneer of strategy as a discipline, defined strategy as the subtle, long-range management of a system over a lengthy period. Some 2500 years ago, Chinese military strategist and philosopher Sun Tzu had already articulated the same idea: "All men can see these tactics whereby I conquer, but what none can see is the strategy out of which victory is evolved."

Examples of change and strategy

In the context of strategic studies, **corporate strategy** refers to everything that takes place on the **holding level.** This could, for example, be the decision to go public (see Uber), the decision to enter brick-and-mortar retail (see Amazon), the decision to rethink a product line (see German meat producer Rügenwalder Mühle's plans to begin offering vegetarian sausages), the decision to participate in a company acquisition (see Monsanto's acquisition by Bayer for 50 billion euros in 2016), the decision to found a joint venture (see the partnership deal signed between Lufthansa and Air China in 2016) or the decision to enter a new market (see the US market launch of car rental company Sixt a few years ago). Below the holding level are various **strategic business units (SBUs)** whose remits are defined by the **business strategy**. Let's take the example of an automotive supplier. The 'Production' unit may decide to outsource parts of its production operations to Romania, the 'Procurement' unit may decide to establish a global sourcing centre, and the 'Marketing' unit may decide to introduce a new customer relationship management (CRM) system for its customers.

All of these examples have one thing in common: they involve changes that are uncomfortable and unwelcome for many involved. Because of this, these changes must be decisively and sustainably anchored among the leaders and employees who will be required to carry them out.

The art of persuasion: communicating with employees

In many cases, your tactical steps should be executed such that they are not apparent to your competitors.

Within your own organization, it's a different story – which is to say, it's vital to take your employees with you. You must always be able to persuade others of what you want to achieve. The Ancient Romans differentiated between **potestas**, the power held by officials by virtue of their office, and **auctoritas**, the natural authority possessed by certain individuals that caused others to want to follow them. If you rely on the power of your office to drive people in your desired direction, 'good' employees will quickly become frustrated. 'Bad' employees will pretend that they have changed, but will actually carry on in much the same vein. So, what's the alternative?

If you want to win support for a new idea, you have three broad options:

- **Money**: this route is readily pursued in, for example, the investment banking sector, where rainmakers are poached from one bank by another. Long term, however, this is a very expensive approach.
- **Violence**: I call this the 'Don Corleone approach' after the legendary *Godfather* character. Faced with a film producer who refuses to sign a contract, Corleone offers his classic pitch: either the producer's brains or his signature will be on the document. Of course, such an approach is highly ethically dubious and almost certain not to result in long-term success.
- **The third way – communication**: In addition to being the obvious choice, this is the only one with the capability to deliver lasting success.

Everyone talks, no-one listens

According to a study by academic Henry Mintzberg, leaders spend 80 per cent of their time engaged in oral communication. At the same time, they perceive 80 per cent of this oral communication to be dull and uninspiring. When we multiply these numbers, we find that **64 per cent of a manager's time is devoted to 'boring' communication in which few to no messages are actually heard.** Little wonder, then, that many initiatives grind to a halt or fail to pick up speed – and ultimately end up as nothing more than a deck of PowerPoint slides in a cupboard.
Bear in mind: it is quite possible that employees will not listen to you or will not understand what you say. If this is the case, they will inevitably also fail to be convinced by what you are suggesting.

Storytelling as a tool

Irrespective of what you want to achieve, you *must* tell a story. **Communication cannot exist in a vacuum**. If you fail to tell a positive story about your project, others will be quick to step in with a negative one. In the best case scenario, your story will not only be a positive one, but the right one for what you intend to do. Rather than compelling employees to do something against their will, a leadership story should bring employees with you. As Sun Tzu recognized thousands of years ago: "To fight and conquer in all our battles is not supreme excellence; supreme excellence consists in breaking the enemy's resistance without fighting."

Whenever you recognize the need for change, you must enable your employees to recognize it too. The best way to do this is through thoughtful communication, ideally in the form of a good story.

1.2 How communication usually happens (and why it goes wrong)

A study by Horváth & Partners showed that in 70 percent of cases where strategies fail, this is not due to the strategy itself, but to implementation – more specifically, to **poor communication**. Kaplan and Norton, meanwhile, found that in some 80 percent of cases where new strategies are implemented, it is not clear what these strategies are supposed to achieve; what, in concrete terms, is supposed to become better. Indeed, **less than five percent** of employees truly understand their organization's strategy at all. You might assume that this is because strategy communication is not a priority at top management level. Actually, the truth is quite the opposite.

An MIT study showed that the effective implementation of strategy tops the list of around 80 challenging responsibilities for CEOs in Asia, the USA and Europe (Sull et al., 2019, p. 74 ff.). How is it possible that something so important is apparently so little understood?

One reason is certainly that strategies are always about a **future vision**, one that inevitably lacks tangibility. Danish physicist Niels Bohr famously observed that "prediction is very difficult, especially about the future." Einstein contented himself with a more pragmatic approach: "I never think of the future – it comes soon enough."

Making the future tangible

The future of the company cannot be shaped by you alone. You need your employees to help you. However, only a very few people will help you out of the goodness of their hearts. In the vast majority of cases, there must be **something 'in it' for others** if they are to aid in realizing your vision. To achieve your goals, they must be willing to make these goals their own.
Even Machiavelli acknowledged that **implementing change is one of the most difficult undertakings of all**, since our brains find it difficult to imagine things that do not yet exist. "There is nothing more difficult to take in hand, more perilous to conduct, or more uncertain in its success, than to take the lead in the introduction of a new order of things," he wrote in his famous work *The Prince (*Machiavelli, 2000, p. 31), demonstrating that the integral and critical nature of change communication is by no means a 21st century phenomenon. "Because the innovator has for enemies all those who have done well under the old conditions," it continues, "and lukewarm defenders in those who may do well under the new. This

coolness arises partly from fear of the opponents, who have the laws on their side, and partly from the incredulity of men, who do not readily believe in new things until they have had a long experience of them."

Reflective change?

Dealing with change is anything but simple; in fact, it is highly complex. Leaders must listen to both external and internal cues and signals.

- **External cues and signals** can come from politics, society, the capital market or from customers.
- **Internal cues and signals** can have their roots in the company cost structure, the corporate culture or the body of employees. All of these require your attention as a leader.

Ideally, companies should respond in a reflective manner. Where the purpose of such a response is to effect change, doing so in a reflective manner brings **real, genuine change**; by the same token, if the purpose of a response is to preserve something, doing so with adequate reflection serves the **meaningful fostering of tradition.** (The latter is a particularly important practice for those small and medium-sized companies that set great store by the stories of their founders.) Regrettably, it happens all too often that such responses are conducted in an unreflective manner, resulting in poorly-conceived, chaotic changes or the arbitrary preservation of certain elements and a resulting perception of rigidity.

Moreover, the speed at which the process occurs is often sufficient to overwhelm the organization completely.

A guaranteed gridlock

It is an unfortunate truth that **the way in which change is communicated in modern companies** is anything but visionary. In many cases, division managers are treated to a tedious board presentation, a flashy music and lights show, team-building exercises in the nearby woods, an evening of boozing and a 'swearing-in' ceremony for the new strategy. The title for such an initiative is easy to assemble: take a reference from the wellness industry or motorsports and a year that is sufficiently far in the future so that nobody remembers it when it inevitably fizzles out. **'Facelift 2020', 'Vision 2030', 'Health Check 2025'** and **'Fit for Future 2028'** all work well in this scenario. If someone does think to ask what happened, you can simply declare it 'still in progress', reissue the title and kick it a bit further down the road with a 'plus' (*Fit for Future 2028 plus*, anyone?).

Approaching 'shake-ups' and 'transitions' with caution

When talking about change, senior management and creative agencies gravitate towards radical-sounding terms such as 'shake-up' and 'transition'. In this regard, I advise caution. Things that are 'in transition' come top of the list for hedge funds and short sellers who make a profit when prices fall. 'Transition' is a state occupied by things and institutions that are unsexy and are most likely doomed to remain so – if they don't disappear forever. Unsightly small towns are often 'in transition', as are failed states, traditional banks and archaic institutions such as churches and universities. **If something is cool, it has no need to be 'in transition'.** Certainly, there is (or was) never much talk of 'transition' with Amazon, *Game of Thrones* or the Rolling Stones.

"I'm fully behind it ..."

It's Monday morning. The PR event is over; the hangover lingers on. Returning to the office, the various division managers do nothing but pass on the board presentation to their teams. "Please, make it happen," they say. It doesn't take a degree in psychology to see that the impact of such change communication is close to zero. Admittedly, as a consultant, I see many managers who at least take the trouble to present the material – yet they often do little more than change the date on the title slide and read off the tedious bullet points by rote, usually mumbling into the screen. "This is the new, pioneering strategy of the board of directors," they assure their team, "and I stand fully behind it." Aside from the fact that this **one-size-fits-all strategy communication** is poorly suited to engendering identification with the project, the **body language** of the ostensibly 'highly motivated' manager usually says something completely different. "My God," it says. "I'm glad I'll be retired next year and won't have to go through this nonsense myself."

Naturally, the **limbic system** in the listener's brain, which is also responsible for **hazard recognition**, senses this discrepancy immediately. "If change is not important to the person in front of me – even though they're getting more money than me – then change is not important to me either." Consequently, employees do not make changes, everything remains the same and the **strategy remains wholly unimplemented.**

The brain says no

The problem with this clinical and uninvolved form of communication is that it **only addresses the cerebral cortex, the rational part of the brain.** This part can also be thought of as the brain's 'CEO'. However, every CEO also has a secretary – in this case the amygdala, also known as the fear centre or 'panic button'. The **amygdala** is much older than the cerebral cortex. Importantly, it has a **lust for stories**, because stories have traditionally always contained best practices for survival. It is responsible for the responses of 'fight', 'flight' and 'fright'. Since, in most presentation settings, we cannot or are not permitted to fight or flee, we are left only with the option of playing dead. We nod along and pretend we agree – but internally, we have already checked out.

The German tabloid newspaper *Bild* deals in the **basic emotions of love, desire, anger, grief, tension and**

fear, which any story capable of appealing to the amygdala should have. We will return to this in the section about storytelling.

Doing the 'right thing', getting the wrong result

If different parts of the company receive different messages and if most employees are not highly motivated to implement them, this can lead to the following scenarios:

- The business units end up heading in different directions, with a lack of any coherent strategy.
- The various business units hinder each other in the achievement of their goals because misunderstandings create conflicts (e.g. when one message is 'reduce costs' and another is 'more time for customers', which are difficult to reconcile).
- Some units simply do what they want. Some head in the direction of the goal, the rest in a different direction entirely.

This is dangerous, because it can lead to all departments **doing their job correctly**, but not doing the right thing **as a whole.**

The difference between 'efficiency' and 'effectiveness'

- To be efficient means to do something right.
- To be effective means to do the right thing.

If we carry out a task correctly but perform it as a small part of a misguided broader approach, a problem arises. As management guru Peter Drucker says, "Even the healthiest business, the business with the greatest effectiveness, can well die of poor efficiency. But even the most efficient business cannot survive, let alone succeed, if it is doing the wrong things, that is, if it lacks effectiveness." (Drucker, 2008, p. 31)

The correct implementation of strategy is considered a top priority by most leaders and senior managers. Even today, however, this is hampered by a lack of practical expertise, with the result that most employees do not understand the point of their organizations' change strategies.

1.3 Change and innovation

Innovation always involves some degree of upheaval and is thus not always popular. Who likes throwing the 'tried and tested' overboard?

Predictions are usually wrong

German Emperor Wilhelm believed that the car was a fad and that the horse would endure. Many years later, Ford Motor founder Henry Ford said: "If I had asked people what they wanted, they would have said faster horses." **It is not, therefore, that the market or the**

customer actively demands innovation. This leads sceptics inside a company to assert that 'nobody wants that – there's simply no market for it.'

In 1895, Lord Kelvin, a mathematician and President of the Royal Society, claimed that "heavier-than-air flying machines are impossible." Thomas Watson, the legendary IBM boss after whom IBM's supercomputer is named, pondered in 1943 that there was a "world market for about five computers." **Innovations are often misjudged.** The Herman Miller office chair was not seen to have any potential; today, it is the world's favourite. Baileys Irish Cream, originally rejected by customer focus groups, is one of the most popular liqueurs on the market – and still the 'drug of choice' for many taking their first sips of alcohol at teenage parties. The Sony Walkman failed every market study: customers couldn't envisage the appeal of listening to music and walking simultaneously. Nobody 'asked' for the iPhone. And almost everyone is now familiar with the humble beginnings of successful authors such as Stephen King, Dan Brown, J.K. Rowling and E. L. James, who experienced hundreds of rejections before finding a publisher.

It is difficult to grapple with the 'new' because it often does not yet exist. At the same time, it is this willingness to engage with change that is so vital for success. With this in mind, there are two options: either the shift to something new is driven proactively from within a company, or it is initiated by external parties. If the latter occurs, this can mean that an external party steals market share from established players – just as Google has stolen market share from traditional advertising providers and mobile navigation devices, Apple has stolen market share from Nokia and Amazon has stolen market share from almost everyone else.

Strategic innovation

A good strategic innovation must meet three criteria:

1. **It must be technically feasible for the company.** Companies often underestimate (or overestimate) their potential. ('No way, we can't, we've never done anything like this before ...')
2. **It must make money.** Business is not a charity event! When the money-making potential of a new innovation is discussed, it is often either talked down or subject to wildly overstated predictions.
3. **It must inspire the customer.** This is the real crux of the matter – and for employees and managers who are reluctant to change, it provides the easy 'killer blow' that is difficult to refute. ('This isn't something our customers want!')

When we consider this third criterion, we realize the remarkable nature of many stories of customer inspiration throughout history. Think back to the beginning of the millennium, when established banking customers suddenly began using PayPal, taxi customers began using apps like 'mytaxi' rather than picking up the phone to the taxi rank, and mobile phone users had no qualms about ditching the ubiquitous Nokia for the iPhone – even though all market research by established companies had shown that customers definitely *didn't* want a touch screen.

Identifying and addressing hazards

The challenge of recognizing innovations often arises from the fact that the **company management does not recognize relevant competitors.** Direct competitors of Coca-Cola, for example, are Pepsi and Fritz-Kola. Indirect competitors could be Bionade or Red Bull, which satisfy a similar need (thirst-quenching), but come from a different category (lemonades/energy drinks). Also in the mix is the **product category** of 'light colas', such as Cola Light and Pepsi Light. All these compete more broadly for market share among 'soft drinks' (including fruit juice), then among the generic grouping of 'general beverages', including water, beer, wine and Starbucks coffee (which, like cola, is a caffeine-containing drink). Finally, all these products complete for customer spending within the overall food & entertainment sector, in which – for example – a visit to the cinema could also vie for customers' cash.

The mistake that managers often make is to look for competitors only in their immediate environment and to forget that competitors or innovations – even those occurring far outside their own category – can become dangerous when they meet **similar customer needs.**

The iPad, for example, has not only destroyed the sales of other tablets, but has helped Netflix to decimate box-office revenue: a large iPad offers a convenient, easy way to download or stream a wide range of films, reducing demand for traditional cinema. The hot breath of competition is closer than you think – and it is vital that this is communicated.

From zero to one

Indirect competitors are much more dangerous because they are not immediately obvious and may come from the periphery of a given industry. Product-based competition exists, for example, between BMW and Mercedes. Needs-based competition exists between BMW and FREE NOW, car2go, Uber etc. What they all have in common is that they satisfy the need for mobility. When the app 'mytaxi' was taken over by Daimler, it was a logical acquisition for the mobility giant to make.

Silicon Valley investor Peter Thiel is the founder of PayPal and was the first outside investor in Facebook. In his book *Zero to One*, Thiel describes the **typical innovation as a step from zero to one**. Starting with a mechanical typewriter and making an electronic one, Thiel theorizes, was a 'step from one to two': making something that already existed a little better. The step from the typewriter to the computer with word processor and printer, however, was a step from zero to one: a genuine innovation. Accordingly, it is not surprising that PCs and printers did not come from the established typewriter manufacturers; nor is it surprising that the iPod, the first device to enable legal music downloads, was developed neither by Walkman and Discman inventor Sony nor by a record company. Thiel also believes that **true innovation often comes from the periphery**, making it difficult for established companies to respond. The next Google will not come from Google, just as the next Apple will not come from Apple (cf. Thiel, 2014, p. 50 ff.).

The new and the familiar

Successful innovations do not necessarily need to turn things upside down. One competitive advantage of successful innovations is that they often **connect the new with the familiar.**

With an iPad, for example, the user turns the pages ('swipes') just like with a physical magazine. They read it on the sofa, not sitting stiffly at a PC. The iPad triggers positive memories of relaxing time at home, not stressful hours at the office in front of a frozen screen. In addition, the swiping motion is reminiscent of a calm, caring physical caress; the screen is effectively 'stroked', causing the brain to register a positive, affectionate response. This is why Apple can afford to position its products less as traditional IT products and more as high-end lifestyle ones – and accordingly, to charge a much higher price.

It pays to think about the customer, not the product

Companies' thinking is often still **more product-oriented than customer-oriented.** If you achieve clarity about who your product is for (and hopefully it is for someone!), you will be better equipped to see which peripheral competitor could make your life difficult and what you can do about it. In this way, you can rally your organization for change.

Rail companies would say that they operate stations, tracks and trains, whereby the latter are hopefully reasonably punctual. However, the effective truth is that, if everything goes smoothly, what they really offer is mobility: the ability to get together with friends, relatives or business partners. Rail brings people together. A film studio makes films, but what it *actually* does it to deal in dreams and entertain people. A pharmaceutical company develops antivirals, but its ultimate goal is to save lives.
With this in mind, the aim of an effective story is a **happy ending that shows what has been improved for the customer** and, ultimately, for the company as well. In addition, it should show why the company can do this better than its competitors and why it is worth the effort of internal change.

Innovation and speed

Success is often a matter of acting **faster than the competition at the right time.** Microsoft's unstoppable rise was in part thanks to IBM's decision, in 1980, to develop its own personal computer in response to Apple's offering (the latter of which, incidentally, would go on to cement the decline of computer maker Digital Equipment Corporation). Since IBM was in a hurry, it turned to Microsoft for an operating system and to Intel for the microprocessor (the 'chip'). Paul Allen and Bill Gates of Microsoft did not yet have an operating system, but immediately saw the opportunity to win a major client and simply pretended they did. With the IBM contract already in place, they quickly (and fortunately) found a developer. The developer programmed the QDOS (Quick and Dirty Operating System), which Microsoft purchased on the spot for 50,000 dollars and sold on to IBM for several million dollars under the name MS-DOS. In addition, Microsoft reserved the right to sell MS-DOS to other PC manufacturers.

This was the beginning of Microsoft's triumphant rise, and shows that often, simple communication can be the key to success. In this case, Microsoft needed simply to say 'yes' at the right moment, despite not yet being perfectly prepared. As BCG founder Bruce Henderson put it: "**The future belongs to the fast.**" This readiness for speed is something that German companies, in particular, still have scope to learn: they are often still working on a prototype as their competitors launch the third edition of a similar product. The audio format MP3, the fax machine and the CD-ROM are all German inventions (the MP3 was developed by the German Fraunhofer

Institute as far back as 1982!), but all of them were marketed and thus monetized by American companies. As I see it, this is also due to a lack of communication expertise. While US managers go to town with big visions, German AGMs are typically taken up with concerns, pessimistic perspectives and questions of regulation and taxation.

Innovation means more

Innovation means more than Silicon Valley, iPhone and Instagram – yet many managers cling doggedly to a narrow vision of innovation as technical gadgets, new apps and flying cars. As a result, they assume there is no need for innovation and thus also no need for the communication of innovation and change. By maintaining this, lazy managers let themselves off the hook – because **innovation can also occur in processes.**

Innovation at Zara, for example, means speed. Zara has an adaptive strategy that consists of responding to fashion trends and rapidly creating dupes of designer clothing from the *haute couture* catwalks in Paris. Scouts discover the latest trends; designers develop the clothes; all production facilities are located in Europe rather than Asia. Shortly afterwards, the shops are stocked with the latest trend products. This works so well that although Zara invests a lot of money in retail units in the best city centre locations, it has never spent a cent on traditional advertising in the entire history of the company.

At Aldi, on the other hand, innovation has traditionally taken the form of low complexity. By restricting itself to around 700 stock-keeping units (SKUs) per store for a period of many years, the administrative burden and logistical complexity of its operations was significantly lower than that of its competitors, some of whom maintained as many as 10,000 to 100,000 SKUs. The advantage – and therefore the customer benefit – was a significantly lower price and yet a higher margin for Aldi than most retailers could achieve. Meanwhile, the accounting system at Chinese refrigerator manufacturer Haier is bold, but successful. Haier employees do not receive a salary in the conventional sense of the word, but are each assigned an individual profit and loss account.

As a result, they can make both large profits and large losses. Haier does not have cost centres; rather, departments such as marketing, accounting, finance and personnel sell their services to employees within the group. The remuneration of employees is made up of a basic salary multiplied by monthly target attainment in % plus a bonus (or deduction) based on the individual profit and loss account (cf. Lafley et al., 2019, p. 60). This certainly wouldn't be everyone's cup of tea, but is ideal for engaged employees who want to be genuine 'entrepreneurs within the company', not just in the platitudes of a CEO's speech.

Innovation – inside and outside

You might already be familiar with the pattern according to which **innovations are taken up by the market.** It corresponds to a Gaussian bell curve, a **standard distribution** of which the first 2.5 percent are the so-called 'innovators': innovation-friendly customers who switch to the new product immediately. The next 13.5 and 34 percent are the 'early adopters' and the 'early majority' respectively. They are followed by the 'late majority' (34 percent) and finally the 'laggards' (16 percent) at the rear.

It is not only these external customers that are important, but your employees – your 'internal customers' – too. These are the people you need to connect with before you can inspire those on the outside. Your task, therefore, is to **internally engender excitement for your project among the majority of your employees.** Innovation without change is impossible. Proactively anchoring change from within an established company is very difficult, but it must be done. If innovation does not come from within, it will come from without – that is, from a competitor or a new entrant from the periphery. By then, it is usually too late.

Particularly when it comes to reacting quickly to innovations (note that, where possible, 'action' is even better than 'reaction'), you should apply a maxim of 'do it yourself or have it done to you'. In other words: 'have lunch or be lunch.' 30

1.4 Newness as a double-edged sword

Former General Electric CEO Jack Welch famously schooled his managers to view the various units of the business as companies they did not yet have in their portfolio, but were looking to buy. Would they actually buy each business unit as they currently found it? The mere fact of having become accustomed to something can skew our perception of it in a positive direction. This notion of bias can also be transferred to other scenarios: for example, a loan advisor who has already arranged several loans for a particular customer will have experienced more losses than an advisor who deals with the customer for the first time, yet the old advisor will likely still be willing to display a greater level of trust. **We do not look too closely at things we know**, preferring instead to give them the benefit of the doubt. **The opposite occurs with new clients: we tend towards suspicion until we feel we know them.**

The desire for things to stay the same

People are creatures of habit and work best when they are not required to deal with new things. This also applies to our everyday lives, in which 45 percent of the activities we carry out are repeated each day. We buy the same brands in the same quantities; we eat the same food (cf. Wood, Neal, 2009). Thanks to consumer research, this phenomenon has been examined far

more closely in relation to human behaviour than it has in relation to corporate strategy and leadership. However, the basic tenet is identical: **'new' is by no means necessarily 'good.'** Many of the companies that have dared to adopt bold new positioning have cautionary tales to tell. In 2009, for example, Tropicana spent millions changing the look and feel of its orange juice for consumers in the USA, with the result that customers no longer recognized the juice and stopped buying it. The brand then had to be 're-repositioned' for many millions more. Ferrero had a similar experience in 2005, when it (unsuccessfully) attempted to change the face of the boy on its children's chocolate packaging. Some years before, in 1985, a new Coca-Cola recipe had caused mass protests in the USA. Under the instruction of legendary CEO Roberto Goizueta, the company was forced to retract to the new recipe and grudgingly apologize to customers.
Such upsets appear destined to keep reoccurring, and companies to keep bashing their heads against the proverbial wall. Not long ago, in April 2019, an announcement by US company Mars about its plan to omit the parmesan sachet from its famous Miracoli pasta packs caused furious uproar. (The fact that the packaging had also undergone a redesign did not exactly make things easier.)

Better the devil you know than the angel you don't

How does this **aversion to the new** – the one you will doubtless have witnessed in response to previous change initiatives – come about? Humans are curious by nature (after all, a previously unknown place might contain new sources of sustenance), but are also inherently distrustful of the unknown. Ever heard the saying 'better the devil you know than the angel you don't'? The reason for this is our **instinct for self-preservation** and the fact that the brain's last 'software update' was about 70,000 years ago. Strictly speaking, therefore, we are creatures of the Stone Age, where the golden rule was that while new things *can* be good (read: can bring new food), they can also bring a lurking sabre-toothed tiger.

In addition, our brain is 80 percent occupied with itself. Art historian Ernst Gombrich noted that **we do not see what we 'see', but rather what we 'know'** (cf. Gombrich, 2002, p. 50). If these internal convictions are stronger than the 'external' PowerPoint slides, the latter are all but doomed to fail.

The fast system and the slow system

In his best-selling book *Thinking, Fast and Slow*, psychologist Daniel Kahneman distinguishes between two systems in the brain: the 'fast' System 1, which carries out up to eleven million processes per second, and the 'slow' System 2, which carries out just 40. System 1 works implicitly, i.e. unconsciously, and System 2 explicitly, i.e. consciously. **System 1 controls 95 percent of our perception and can quickly be tempted to make sweeping judgements.** When we buy something, for example, 70 percent of our purchase decisions are made directly at the point of sale and not before.

System 1 is also the older and therefore more powerful part of the brain, and can do things that the slower System 2 cannot. It is via System 1, for example, that we recognize a face that we have not seen for 20 years. It is System 1 that lets us notice a new carpet in our favourite holiday apartment without being able to say the colour of the old one. It is System 1 that enables us to recognize our grandmother in sunglasses, an ability that still eludes even the most sophisticated face recognition technology. It is System 1 that links the colour red with Coca-Cola, a connection very much desired by Coca-Cola and which it has achieved through decades of billion-pound advertising.

Further issues arise when the systems try to interact – which is to say, we are *not* capable of multitasking, no matter how often this may be claimed or expected of us. If a new thought is activated in the slow System 2, it is impossible for us to service this and the current thought at the same time. Either the current thought is 'over' – replaced by the new one – or the new thought is outsourced to the fast System 1. **The issue here is that System 1 processes thoughts differently, placing far more emphasis on emotions than the rational Sys-**

tem 2. Moreover, the level of correlation between the two systems is too low to be of meaningful use, with the correlation coefficient (the degree of mutual interrelation) standing at just 24 percent (cf. Scheier, Held, 2014, p. 78 ff.). In the context of change, this can mean just one thing: **that your change communication must keep impulsive System 1 in mind!**

Thinking and possessing

If you make your change story too drawn-out and unwieldy, you are asking the brain to think. Thinking – especially the kind of thinking for which System 2 is responsible – is frowned upon by the brain. The brain accounts for just two percent of body weight, but consumes 20 percent of the body's energy. Thus, careful budgeting is the order of the day, since any energy the brain wastes in thinking is diverted away from reproduction (and thus from the survival of the species). From an evolutionary and biological point of view, anything less than **consistent thriftiness in thinking** makes no sense at all.

Logically, then, **our brain loves things it knows:** if we already trust a piece of information, we are spared the process of weighing-up and thinking. Campaigning to be re-elected chancellor in the German federal election in 2013, Angela Merkel won the debate against fellow candidate Peer Steinbrück by telling the audience, "Sie kennen mich" ("You know me"). Detergent brand Persil deployed a similar tactic in its old German advertisements: “Da weiß man, was man hat” (“You know what you’re getting”). Psychologists call this phenomenon the **endowment effect**, which means that we regard things we have as more valuable than things we don’t have. This is the reason why we are reluctant to sell stocks, even if they are deep in the red, and why we often cling to things that actually have no future, or continue to invest in projects that will never pay off. “I’ve invested so much, I can’t back out now,” we tell ourselves – although, rationally speaking, that is exactly what we should be doing.

In a famous experiment by Daniel Kahneman, students were asked what they would pay for a particular coffee cup. On average, the amount was three euros. Another group of students received the coffee cup as a gift and were asked how much they would sell it for. The answer was seven euros – over 100 percent higher than the value attributed by the other group! The coffee cup was the same; it was only the fact that it already belonged to the students that raised its value in their eyes (The experiment is described in Kahneman et al., 1990, pp. 1325–1348). **What we have and know is thus always more valuable to us than what we don’t**, and the judgement of whether or not we like the ‘new’ takes place unconsciously in more than 80 percent of cases. Brain researcher Gerhard Roth summed it up succinctly in a recent interview with me: “Consciousness is just a PR campaign by the brain to make you think that you have something to say.”

Uninspiring talk leads to worse implementation

When it comes your change story, therefore, you must **make it as easy as possible for the brain of the person you are talking to.** You must address not only their rational side, but their emotions, too. Since System 2 is often overburdened, information processing is frequently 'outsourced' to System 1. If your change story is not emotional enough, it will be eliminated from further consideration. To make things even trickier: the brain, which is designed to deal with its old and known world, will find any excuse at all not to engage with an unknown, new world – especially if it is not only uncertain, but poorly communicated.

Moreover, when it comes to System 1, a poorly communicated change story (remember the example from section 1.2?) can achieve the opposite effect to the one intended. If a speaker reels off a passage of text in an apathetic fashion, the listener – who is processing it in System 1 – thinks, "Great! I can be just as half-hearted in implementing it!"

This correlation is so significant that it is possible to measure it. To do this, Yale University psychologist John A. Bargh asked one group of students to write an essay on sport and one on retirement homes. As is so often the case with such psychological tests, the results of the written task were not really the point. What he was really wanted was to measure the time the students took to travel from the lecture hall to the university exit once they had finished writing. The result was that those who had written about retirement homes travelled significantly slower than their counterparts in the other group (cf. Bargh, 2008).

Giving System 2 a chance

To finish, some good news: **decisions in the cerebral cortex are made by System 2.** As a result, System 2 can overrule System 1 – but only if it wants to. Moreover, due to its frequent state of overload, System 2 regularly recruits the help of System 1 – including when processing change strategies. Thus, such strategies often face two problems:

1. The new thing to be implemented is not, by its nature, to System 1's liking.
2. The strategy is conveyed in a boring and unemotional way, which also produces an undesirable reaction from System 1.

The good news is that the second problem, at least, is one you can counteract. How to tell your change story in a way that appeals to System 1 will be explained in the next section!

Before you begin drafting your change story, there are four vital aspects to consider: 30

- ***The goal must be clear. Strategy is the path to the goal. In this context, the goal is to create a new or better company. Thus, strategy is also the path to change.***

- ***Conventional strategy communication can face a number of stumbling blocks. In particular, it is quite common for your listeners to believe that you do not genuinely endorse the strategy. The problem is that if employees then refuse to participate, the strategy will fail whether you endorse it or not.***
- ***Change is not a nice-to-have, but a necessity for survival. It is not only innovations from within the company that are decisive for its survival, but those on the outside, too. Innovation only works through change – and change must be successful in order for it to have any purpose at all.***
- ***Employees are not impatient for change. On the contrary: our Stone Age brains take a negative attitude towards the unfamiliar. This makes it even more important for your change strategy to have an emotional dimension: one that will address the impulsive and sceptical part of the brain that is usually responsible for issuing judgements.***

30 MINUTES

2. The change story

It is far from a given that our brains will respond enthusiastically to new things. The reason is that our instinct for self-preservation perceives reality as more dangerous than it often is and, as a result, the brain sees the 'new' as a danger rather than an opportunity. It also important to note that the brain uses stories to make sense of reality. Thus, in order to make your change strategy as impactful as possible, it is vital that you tell a story.

2.1 A problem for every solution

In many cases, those in charge of change projects fail to clearly state why change is necessary – a problem that begins with their choice of **language, which is often very abstract.** "We need to increase shareholder value," they say, when what they *should* be saying is: "The more profits we make, the more secure your jobs are and the sooner we can increase your salaries."

A world without villains is not a credible one

Similarly, it is **often the case that change projects 'sell' a solution to a problem that is not readily apparent to others.** This is problematic, because we as humans need to understand a problem in order to agree that it is worth working towards a solution (or, in story terms, a 'happy ending'). We believe a story with a villain much more readily than one without. As Alfred Hitchcock put it: "The more successful the villain, the more successful the picture." Again, it is our zealous instinct for self-preservation that is responsible for this phenomenon. We believe that if we overestimate danger, it cannot harm us; if we underestimate it, however, the sabre-toothed tiger might just have chance to pounce.

In light of this, it is no coincidence that, according to anthropologist Paul Ekman, there are **five basic negative emotions**, but only one neutral and one positive one.

These basic negative emotions are **contempt, anger, sadness, fear and disgust. Surprise** is neutral, and only **joy** is positive.

The pain of (not) acting

Due to our propensity to assign greater weight to the negative than the positive, the amygdala, which is located in the limbic system of the brain, rates stories without a 'bad guy' as untrustworthy and even as treacherous, since they attempt to present a hostile reality as harmless. **If there is no villain, our brain creates its own.** This negative force might, for example, take the form of the generally unappealing nature of change, the possibility of job cuts or the effort involved in repositioning the company. Think of it like this: if a company does not differentiate its services sufficiently of its own accord, a customer will carry out the differentiation for themselves, using price as the main criterion. In the case of a company change project, it is the employee's brain that performs this 'differentiation' – and it settles on a villain to make the story make sense.

Neuromarketing research has found that the 'pain' a customer experiences when paying for a product, i.e. when spending their hard-earned cash, is activated by a region of the brain known as the insula (incidentally, the same entity that is responsible for toothache). When dealing with change, the insula works in exactly the same way. **If the pain of change appears to be**

greater than the problem it is solving, the change will be rejected wholesale.

Only the positive needs to be proven

It is because of the above-described phenomenon that budding authors in thriller-writing workshops are advised to create their villains first, since the villain shapes what is required of the hero. If a story lacks a credible villain, the hero is rendered redundant from the off. The same applies for change projects; that is to say, if there is no clear problem to be solved, the change strategy is deemed superfluous. Employees (rightly) ask: "Why should we change anything if everything is fine already?" Compounding this is the fact that we are much **more willing to believe the bad than the good**, which means the standard of evidence required for negative things is much lower than for positive ones. If I told you I was the best football player in the world, you would almost certainly not believe it. If, however, I told you I was the *worst*, this would appear a lot more reasonable. The final factor is that we are much more likely to share negative experiences than positive ones. If a customer is satisfied with a product, they will recommend it to an average of three friends; if they are not satisfied, they will complain to nine.

United by the negative

In a film-based experiment, viewers from different cultures were connected to an EEG machine to examine the extent to which their brains responded in harmony when viewing the material. While watching footage of New York, five percent of their brains responded in a more or less equal fashion; for a comedy, it was 18 percent. Different cultures have different views on what constitutes humour. Much greater levels of agreement were seen with Hitchcock's grisly shower murder scene in *Psycho*, to which some 65 percent of participants exhibited a similar brain response. (A description of this experiment can be found at www.hassonlab.com.) The negative unites us because it activates the above-described **instinct for self-preservation:** the innate propensity for paranoia whose purpose is to prolong our lives. Our limbic system is built on the motto 'better a pessimist who stays alive than an optimist who has perished.'

The 'secretary' and the 'bouncer' of the brain

Communication in organizations is often highly technical and seeks to address 'System 2', the rational – but slower – part of the brain. At the heart of System 2 lies the cerebral cortex – an evolutionarily young part of the brain, but one which is ultimately afforded the final say on rational matters. Unfortunately, that's not all there is to it. I have previously described the cerebral cortex as the 'CEO of the brain' – and as we all know, every CEO has a secretary. In the case of the brain, the 'secretary' is the amygdala. To make things even trickier, a third part of the brain, the **hypothalamus**, acts both as a '**doorman**' and a 'commanding officer', transmitting commands from the CEO to the body ("Command to the hand: sign the contract!"). At some 70,000 years old, both the amygdala and hypothalamus are, in an evolutionary sense, significantly older than the CEO, and are drawn to stories in which a villain (a problem) must be eliminated in order for a happy ending (a solution) to be achieved. This is because, by their nature, stories that follow this pattern reveal **tips for survival in a hostile world.** If no such story is provided, the secretary and the bouncer will block the information long before it lands at the CEO's door.

30 *Many change initiatives come to nothing because employees simply do not see the point. For them, it is unclear what is to be made better and what 'villain' is to be overcome. As such, before you propose a solution, it is vital that you outline the problem to be solved. A world without problems – without villains – is not credible for the human brain.*

2.2 Change cannot exist in a vacuum

When it comes to change projects, managers often fail to reckon sufficiently with the fact that their own story is far from the only one. Rather, numerous stories will be circulating in the heads of employees. Such stories might claim that the whole affair is doomed to failure, that the same thing has been heard a thousand times, or that employees simply need to hang fire for another two months and wait for the project to inevitably fizzle out. Most dangerously, a story might claim that the change process is inherently unfavourable for the company and its employees. **Understanding is the exception**; misunderstanding is the rule. As Prussian general and military strategist Helmuth von Moltke put it: "An order that can be misunderstood will be misunderstood."

In the end, one party or the other will seize control of the narrative – you, or the blockers of change. Former US Secretary of Defence Donald Rumsfeld aptly observed that if a government does not step up and govern, someone else will. With communication, it's no different. Whether **you tell a convincing story or leave a gap for someone else to do so**, a story *will* be told.

Some years ago, a group of students in California sparked panic with a petition to "ban DHMO", a substance they alleged to be "everywhere and highly dangerous." The whole thing was of course, no more than a science-based prank: dihydrogen monoxide is two parts hydrogen and one part oxygen, better known as 'H_2O' or 'water'. It was not a threat at all, but was readily perceived as one due to its dangerous-sounding name.

How to neutralize 'anti-stories'

If you want your change story to cut through the noise, you will need to fight the obstacles and 'anti-stories' that have been accepted as true in the brains of those you wish to convince.

A 2008 experiment showed just how strongly such **beliefs** can influence us on a subliminal level. In the experiment, 341 test subjects were required to undertake what they believed was a reaction test and to press a button when they saw a signal. The purpose of the test was ostensibly to measure their eye-hand coordination. As is often the case with such experiments, the actual matter under investigation was something entirely different. For a period of microseconds, one third of the test group were shown the IBM logo, the next third a blank image and the final third the Apple logo. The participants were then given a creativity task in which they were asked to name as many ideas as they could for making use of a set of stones.

The group that had been subliminally influenced by the IBM logo had an average of 5.5 ideas for using the stones, while the no-logo group and the Apple logo group had 6.1 ideas and 7.3 ideas respectively. In this case, it appears that the value proposition of the respective companies was so powerful that both the authoritative sobriety of IBM ("Nobody gets fired for buying IBM") and the creativity attributed to Apple in 2008 ("Think different") had perceptible effects on creativity and the performance of the task (see Fitzsimons et al., 2008, p 21-35). This interesting experiment also indicates that generally, humans come **with a range of preconceived beliefs.** If your company has already experimented with various changes of strategy and found that most of them remained unrealized, you can be sure this phenomenon is alive and well in your organization. In such cases, you should remember the words of Professor Peter Kruse in his famous German-language business talk "8 Regeln für den totalen Stillstand" ("8 rules for total gridlock"). "In companies like yours, employees view change like a flu in the company," he said. "It lasts 14 days if you take medication or two weeks if you don't. Either way, they believe they just need to wait a bit and everything will return to normal." (See https://www.youtube.com/watch?v=Ug83sF_3_Ec&t=60s)

Unofficial stories: dealing with gossip

Given the above, it is vital that you **unambiguously identify the villain and do not permit the development of a vacuum.** You might, for example, say: "We have two hard years ahead of us in order to drive competitors out of our territory. It won't always be a bed of roses. But afterwards, we'll be the successful company that we once were and wish to be again." If, on the contrary, you overlook the need for a villain or problem, employees will create a story and villain of their own. This story might go something like: "The evil board of directors and their equally evil management consultants want an excuse to get rid of us loyal, hard-working staff."

This is not a good starting point for a turnaround. In addition, it creates a downward spiral whereby employees are even more predisposed to believe the negative over the positive in the future. Once this situation arises, **those leading the change have all but lost control of the narrative** (since, at the end of the day, it is the recipient who decides how a message is received).

Everyone knows how quickly rumours – "I think they want to close the whole department!" – spread within a company. In his book *The Tipping Point,* Malcolm Gladwell cites three factors that contribute to tipping the balance in favour of hearsay (Gladwell, 2008, p. 29):

- First, the **law of the few**, which acknowledges that it doesn't take many people to spread a rumour in a company.
- Secondly, the 'stickiness' factor: the degree to which **the story sticks.** Rumours and stories are always memorable. By contrast, dry strategy presentations and rebuttals of rumours by corporate communications go in one ear and out the other.
- The third and final factor is the power of **context.** While strategy presentations contain abstract diagrams with little apparent relevance for employees' day-to-day working lives, gossip frames the information in such a way that the effects on employees are thrown into sharp relief.

Think of the tabloid press, whose existence is rooted in the dictum that **people like to read about people more than they do about things.** This message appears not (yet) to have filtered through to the world of corporate communications, which gravitates towards the heavy use of bar charts, diagrams and bullet points. Rumour merchants in the company are afforded free reign to seize control, and the unofficial story becomes: "*We* are affected. *Our* department is to be closed down. *Our* future is in danger."

In the past, humans shared best practices for survival in the form of stories around a campfire. Today, the **modern campfires** that play host to the spread of gossip and rumours are part of every organization. They are the kitchens and canteens; the smoking areas where the smoke of rumours mingles with that of hastily-smoked cigarettes. If a board of managers invites its top young talent to a discussion behind the scenes, this is still referred to in German as a 'Kamingespräch' ('fireside chat'), though there is (usually) no actual fireplace to be seen.

If unofficial gossip is 'stickier' because it better matches the structure of an effective story, your own strategy story will fall on deaf ears. What's more, denying such unofficial stories – refuting them as untrue – will be equally futile, if not outright counterproductive. The effect is similar to that seen when you tell a child not to slam the door: it is merely slammed shut with even greater force. Just as our brains cannot deal with a vacuum, **they can't do anything with a 'no'.**

No matter who tells it, a story will be told

Change cannot exist in a vacuum, which means that a story must always be told. This leaves you with a choice: either you tell a 'good' (positive) story about your project, or you leave space for others to tell a 'bad' one. Be aware that in forming their anti-stories, employees will often afford themselves much greater creative licence than you give yourself. Consider Germany's Dresdner Bank, which, following a clumsy takeover by Allianz in 2001 and hundreds of hasty change initiatives, earned itself the unofficial internal slogan "Bad doesn't have to be cheap". The bank has been defunct since 2009.

30 *You might believe that a good change story is unnecessary. While you're perfectly entitled to think so, the problem in practice is that you cannot stop employees telling their own stories to fill the gap. To make things even worse, such stories spread like wildfire as a result of the propensity for gossip and rumours in businesses. In the end, no matter who tells it, a story will be told: the positive one you want to be heard, or the negative one that comes hot off the rumour mill.*

2.3 From strategy to story

So far, we have learned that there is *always* a story – whether the positive one told *by* you, or the negative one that is told *about* you. This is the bad news. However, there is also good news: namely **that stories can be planned** – just like infrastructure projects, restructuring projects and expansion strategies – so as to help you maintain ultimate control. Thriller novels and Netflix films are by no means created in the way many of us might imagine – with a muse revealing themselves to the author after hours of deep contemplation – but by hard graft in the writer's room and diligent planning. In business, too, you must put in the necessary work to tell an effective story. The old Hollywood adage "There's no business without show business" is as true for presentations as it is for anything else!

Stories at their simplest

What makes a good story? First and foremost, a good story makes the listener a part of the action.

> **In the words of Confucius...**
> According to Confucius, there are three ways of acquiring knowledge:
> - By wisdom, which is noblest.
> - By imitation, which is easiest.
> - By experience, which is the bitterest.

A good story draws the listener in. When we see James Bond suffer at the hands of a villain, we identify more strongly with him as the hero. Our 'cuddling hormone', oxytocin, is activated. In a change story, we share the highs and lows of the protagonist in just the same way. A good story illustrates what obstacles need to be overcome and why it is worth our while to overcome them. Such a story must make clear:

1. That the listener needs to make a change.

Like a thriller, a change story features a villain to be defeated. Here, it is vital to convey that **not acting is not an option**. The costs of not acting – letting the villain win – must be higher than the costs of acting, i.e. participating in the change or transformation. This creates a situation in which there is no acceptable alternative to implementing your project.

2. That the listener needs to work with you, the teller of the story, to effect this change.

One character is chosen to bring about the happy ending in just about every novel or film: just think of Luke Skywalker, Bilbo Baggins or Jack Ryan. You, as the storyteller, must show the other person that **you are the 'James Bond' of change!**

3. That the listener must do something *now*.

Every good thriller has a ticking time bomb – one that is set to explode sooner rather than later. In Dan

Brown's *Angels & Demons*, the Vatican is at risk of explosion in just 30 minutes' time. In the adventures of James Bond, the time fuse is more likely to be set to five minutes than five hours. **Drama and urgency** in a change story encourage the listener to act promptly – and thus to accomplish even complex transformation projects in a swift and goal-oriented manner.

The advantages of stories

Stories work better than facts because they can do some things that facts cannot.

- **Stories activate empathy:** We share in the experiences of others as if they were our own.
- **Stories allow us to experience things we haven't experienced in real life:** We see this with crime novels, thrillers and fantasy epics like *Star Wars, The Lord of the Rings* or *Game of Thrones.*
- **Stories are persuasive**: The basic structure of a story is burned into our human brain. As a result, information that is framed in a story structure is more likely to be perceived as credible. According to author and psychologist Daniel Kahneman, we look at reality and turn what we see into a story. If that story rings true, it is believed by the brain.
- **We learn through stories**: Hundreds and thousands of years ago, our ancestors relayed best practices for survival in story form. Still nowadays, our natural inclination is to use stories to structure our reality. As soon as we recognize that we are listening

to a story, our ears prick up. We are primed to expect a piece of information that will help us survive in a hostile world.

The villain of the piece

I am often asked why a story needs a villain ("Doesn't this make it far too negative?"). While this idea is not without merit, it is impossible to ignore the fact that a reality without villains is simply not credible. Think of interesting stories or jokes you have heard in the past. When we hear such things, we instinctively look for the so-called **'punchline': the part of the story where something happens contrary to expectations or goes wrong.** In other words, we look for the **conflict.** Suppose I were to tell you the following story:

- I went to Berlin's central station.
- Then, I got on the train to Hanover.
- In Hanover, I met with a customer.
- We had a coffee together.
- Then, I drove to Cologne...

Do you sense it? Yes: the conflict is missing. We expect to hear something unexpected or out of the ordinary – that the train was late, the customer forgot the appointment or the meeting was supposed to be in Hamburg, not Hanover. When we are subjected to a story that lacks a punchline, we often feel a degree of irritation: it is boring to listen to, lacks interest and wastes our time and attention. At most, the wastage associated with the above example would be a few moments of the listener's time. In the business world, however, where the cost of failed leadership communication can run into the tens of millions or more, it is quite astonishing that we content ourselves with boring stories: those that lack suspense, punchlines and decent villains to boot. It seems clear that something, somewhere has gone awry. When CEO Zhang Ruimin restructured the then almost-insolvent Chinese refrigerator manufacturer Haier in 1984, he chose the strongest 'punchline' available. Haier had been forced into the free market by Deng Xiaoping's programme of reforms, whereupon it emerged that the 'white goods' that Haier produced – while living up to the 'white' part of their name – were anything but high-quality. Some customers even drew sardonic parallels between the white of the refrigerators and the status of white as a traditional east Asian colour of mourning. Seeking to turn things around, Zhang Ruimin stood in front of the assembled staff and took a hammer to the old refrigerators, asking his employees to destroy the goods with him. This marked the start of Haier's legendary comeback. Today, the company holds a global market share of 14 percent in white goods such as washing machines and fridges.

What types of stories can organizations tell?

The hammer used by Ruimin to smash the refrigerators is now housed in a museum in Beijing. As such, the fridge-smashing and subsequent turnaround of Haier represent a typical **origin story**: the story of how a company came to be. Companies seeking to tell their own origin story might ask which exotic corners of the world their product or raw material comes from, or, as in Haier's case, which date or event ushered in the company's ascent.

Another category is the **inventor story**, which, as its name suggests, concerns the inventor and invention that started the company and how the invention came about. Mobility giant Daimler portrayed its inventor story in an advertisement with the slogan "Das Beste oder nichts" ("The best or nothing"), in which pioneering engineer Gottfried Daimler was seen working at his desk.

User stories tell of the interesting people who have bought a product or used a service. The line between user stories and celebrity advertising is fluid; in the latter case, however, it is usually the celebrity and not the company who sticks in the audience's mind, so caution is advised. In the context of a change strategy, celebrity advertising can be compared to a costly kick-off event (complete with music star or TV presenter) and a subsequent anticlimactic roll-out in which nothing is achieved at all. Costs are high; impact is zero.

In contrast to user stories, **usage stories** talk about the usual and unusual ways in which the product or service is used. This is one of the most interesting types of story, since it involves a sort of 'hero's quest' (customer journey) to show which problems can be better solved by the product or service at hand.

The three elements of a good story

Like any good story, an effective strategy story should consist of three parts:

1. The story of the storyteller

A good personal story talks of the other projects for which you have, so to speak, 'pulled the chestnuts out of the fire'. In doing so, it gives the other person's brain the feeling that you can be relied upon. Generally speaking, if your change project does not involve a product or a strategy that can be portrayed in concrete terms (because the strategy is too meta or abstract), **you yourself must be the strategy.**

2. The elevator pitch

The first impression is the one that counts. Those who do not succeed in positioning and differentiating themselves in a succinct fashion at the outset will find it difficult to do so in the further course of the project. Remember: if you don't tell a story, others will.

3. The persuasive story

For each solution you offer, you must first outline a problem. Just as any good story needs a villain, **a strategy must solve a problem**; otherwise, it has no raison d'être and nobody will put themselves out to achieve it. In sales, for example, the greatest pain a customer can experience is a high price. Your job is to counter this with an even greater villain: the customer's problem, which will remain a problem for as long as the customer fails to make a change or does not buy your product. The problem could even be that without this change, the customer's company is doomed to failure. Generally, if you sell a solution without first stating the problem, you will at best achieve minimal agreement and at worst, none at all. It goes without saying that change will be almost impossible as a result.

The story code

As we learned earlier, there is certain story structure – a 'code' – that is burned into the human brain. We use it both to tell ourselves stories and to make sense of reality. Good stories take the form of a '**four-note chord**' with the four consistent basic elements: **situation, disaster, turning point and happy ending.**

The code of a good story:

- **Situation:** Where do we stand as a company? Where are we headed?
- **Disaster:** What is preventing us from reaching our goal? Who or what is the 'villain' that threatens us?
- **Turning point:** What are the sacrifices we need to make: those that may hurt in the short term, but will make us successful in the long term?
- **Happy ending:** What is the glorious future that awaits? Why is it worth the effort required?

Before you tell a persuasive story to demonstrate the value of a change, you can – as previously mentioned –

tell a **'story of the storyteller'** that shows why you deserve to be believed. Just like a change story, this should focus on an **obstacle you have overcome in the past**. In the following example, we look at the path Arnold Schwarzenegger took from bodybuilder to Hollywood star.

- **Situation**: *After appearing in 'Hercules in New York' and 'Conan the Barbarian', Arnold Schwarzenegger felt it was time for a serious role. He auditioned for various acting agencies.*
- **Disaster**: *The results were disappointing. Even though the agencies had liked 'Conan', they did not see Schwarzenegger as a candidate for a serious acting career. Again and again, he was told that his movements were too robotic and wooden: a style of movement he had picked up from years of posing during his bodybuilding career.*
- **Turning point**: *At that time, it just so happened that James Cameron was looking for a leading actor for 'The Terminator', a film about a machine from the future that looked like a human being. By chance, he came across Schwarzenegger.*
- **Happy ending**: *As a human being who acted like a machine, Schwarzenegger was the perfect casting choice for a machine that acted like a human being. While 'Conan' had had its fair share of success, 'The Terminator' was what ushered in Schwarzenegger's career as a Hollywood superstar.*

As you have probably noticed by now, the storyteller's story is built around **a disadvantage that later yields an advantage**. As such, it follows the pattern of the persuasive story. The following is another example of a storyteller's story, this time that of Amazon Web Services (AWS):

- **Situation**: *At the end of the 1990s, Jeff Bezos found himself needing to build a massive IT infrastructure to handle the growing demand for online commerce.*
- **Disaster**: *In the period before Christmas, when many customers were ordering gifts, Amazon was required to provide a much greater level of infrastructure than it needed for the rest of the year.*
- **Turning point**: *Because, in those days, money was tight, Bezos decided to rent out this IT infrastructure when it wasn't needed. It was booked out for much of the year. While people were on holiday at Christmas, business demand was lower, so it was freed up for Amazon to handle its Christmas orders.*
- **Happy ending**: *AWS is now market leader in the rental of cloud computing and storage.*

So-called **start-up stories** exhibit a comparable structure. Apple, now one of the most valuable companies in the world, was long viewed as the 'start-up story' of Steve Jobs, who experienced his very own disaster and turning point. Following the company's humble beginnings in a garage, Jobs was forced to resign from the company in the 1990s. He later returned as a heroic lost son and oversaw the subsequent meteoric rise of Apple thanks to the iPod, iPhone and iPad.

Another example of a classic start-up story is that of skin care brand La Mer, whose signature cream now retails for hundreds of euros per pot. Its creator, rocket scientist Dr Max Huber, had suffered burns to the face during a fuel experiment. Some twelve years later, he made the chance discovery that certain types of algae were effective at smoothing his skin. In a 'happy ending', he used these specially fermented algae not only to heal his own skin, but to create his world-famous formula.

There is some disagreement as to whether this story is one hundred percent true. While La Mer is certainly more expensive than other creams, it is not demonstrably better. Nevertheless, the story has been highly effective. As a general rule, our Stone Age brains are suspicious of those who ask something difficult of us **without having proven that they have, so to speak, pulled the chestnuts out of the fire themselves**. Consider the following statement from a famous sea-captain, who alleged never to have encountered trouble at sea:

"But in all my experience, I have never been in any accident ... or any sort worth speaking about. I have seen but one vessel in distress in all my years at sea. I never saw a wreck and never have been wrecked nor was I ever in any predicament that threatened to end in disaster of any sort."

This **'fair-weather captain'** was E. J. Smith, captain of the RMS Titanic, speaking in 1907. In light of the tragic sinking of the Titanic in 1912, it might be wondered whether it was a good idea to entrust such a person with the command of a ship at all. You will no doubt remember the unenthusiastic presentations of the division managers in chapter 1.2, from which it was difficult to believe that they truly stood behind their change stories. A further **example of the negative effects of unconvincing leadership** is shown in the 1997 film *From Dusk till Dawn*, in which George Clooney's character, Seth, is challenged by one of his crew (because Seth wants to "break a bottle" over a "melon head"): "Before we stepped in here, you told all of us to be cool. That means you, too." "I never said do what I do – I said do what I say," Seth replies.

A practical example

Imagine that a large consultancy – let's call it 'East Coast Consulting', or 'ECC' – has to date worked with many large companies in Germany, but now needs to win new customers from the small and medium-sized enterprise sector in the north of the country. This is because some of the existing large customers are being forced to switch their business to other providers for reasons of compliance. In order for this new strategy to be a success, ECC's consultants need to be persuaded of its merits. ECC has two smaller competitors and one larger competitor in the region. For customers in the north, the most important considerations are globalization (that is, they want a partner that is capable of operating on a global level) and digitalization. By awarding points to the three alternatives (A1, A2 and A3) according to a predefined set of criteria, prospective clients can take into account all important considerations in parallel. In addition to the global and digital know-how mentioned above, these clients also expect a local presence and a well-developed sense for the needs and concerns of SMEs.

	A1	**A2**	**A3**
Criteria	Small competitors	Large competitor	ECC
Local	Yes	No	Yes
Global	No	Yes	Yes
Digital	No	Yes	Yes

When the information is evaluated in this way, it becomes obvious that only ECC can deliver everything that matters to the prospective clients. Small competitors are 'local', but not global or digital enough. ECC's large competitor is also global, but does not deem it necessary to have offices in the north of Germany. Of course, before you tell this story, you must be certain that your company actually meets all these criteria; otherwise, employees will rightly question the premise. Storytelling is not simply making up a fairy-tale!

In this case, the **persuasive story** could go something like this:

- **Situation**: *We at East Coast Consulting have been very successful in working with large DAX companies in Germany in recent years.*
- **Disaster**: *However, we have recently lost some large contracts due to new processes in our clients' purchasing departments. Due to the length of time for which we have been working with some of the companies, their supervisory boards and purchasing departments have insisted on a 'change of scene' for compliance reasons. This has forced us to look at other potential customers.*
- **Turning point**: *SMEs could be an interesting opportunity for us, particularly in the northern region of Germany. The companies there are almost as global and digitally friendly as their DAX counterparts. Our major competitor is as global and digital as we are, but has no offices in the north of the country. By contrast, the local agencies have specific SME know-how – as do we – but are less well-placed to advise on digitalization or global affairs.*
- **Happy ending**: *Our global expansion and digitalization expertise makes us the best possible option for small and medium-sized businesses in the northern region of Germany. Time to get started!*

Of course, the above is only intended as an illustrative example; the final story would likely be much richer in

detail and **examples**. The key point to remember is that any major strategy must not only be announced in a top-down fashion, but adapted to the individual profit centres (in this case, the northern region of Germany).

There is no such thing as change in a vacuum. If you fail to tell an effective change story, others will swoop in to fill the gap. In addition, because the human brain naturally assigns more credence to the negative than the positive, the anti-story that prevails will likely be a negative one. To prevent this, take the following steps: 30

- ***Develop a change story with a clear 'villain': a problem for which finding a solution is worth taking on the pain of change.***
- ***When building a story, follow the structure 'situation → disaster → turning point → happy ending'. This chimes neatly with the pre-programmed story code in our brain and ensures that the audience will remember it.***
- ***As the storyteller, you must be credible. Thus, tell a 'story of the storyteller' that demonstrates how you have solved a problem in the past. This groundwork gives your persuasive story the best possible chance of sticking.***

30 MINUTES

3. Allies for your change project

In the previous chapters, we learned that you need to know where your journey is going, what you want to achieve and what story you are going to tell. However, it is not enough to simply 'announce' a strategy, even if you do so in the form of a story. **In addition, consider that there will be (small or large) groups of influential individuals who are for or against it.** Identifying these people and getting them on board – or at least minimizing their potential harmful effects – is essential. What's more, this must be done *before* you set off to deliver your big speech at the company leadership meeting.

3.1 The stakeholder matrix

Your job is to find out who the relevant stakeholders are and what makes them tick. If you fail to do so, your strategy will not be implemented in a uniform fashion throughout the hierarchy. Instead, you will have a cacophony of a hundred different strategies and opinions and will encounter frustrated managers, employees and, ultimately, customers. The most important questions to ask in this regard are **'How do stakeholders view the project?'** and **'How much power do they actually have?'**.

What matters in change projects

In his book *Leading Change*, John Kotter defined the eight cardinal errors that occur in change processes. Three of these relate to storytelling. They are:

- **Not establishing a great enough sense of urgency**; in other words, failing to make clear that the bomb is already ticking.
- **Lacking an attractive vision**, which has the knock-on effect that the goal of the strategy is unclear. For the audience, this means that there is no happy ending worth fighting for.
- **Undercommunicating the vision**, or failing to tell a good story.

Two of the errors mentioned by Kotter relate to stakeholder engagement. They are:

- Not creating a **powerful enough guiding coalition**.
- Failing to remove **obstacles** to the new vision.

Kotter's remaining three errors focus on implementation, namely: failing to systematically plan for (and create) short-term wins, declaring victory too soon and failing to anchor the changes in the corporate culture.

Four main stakeholders

It is clear, then, that stakeholders play a crucial role. Stakeholders in a company can be divided into four groups:

1. The gossipmonger

First, there are the gossipmongers. These often take the form of employees who have been **part of the furniture** for 30 years or more and are now required, for example, to stop stamping forms and start using an iPad. For them, the request alone constitutes a significant grievance. In addition, they are usually on the brink of full or partial retirement and thus do not see the point in helping to bring about change.

- **Attitude**: Negative
- **Influence**: Low (but exist in large numbers, thus great potential for gossip, rumours and anti-stories)

2. The yes-man

Next, there are the yes-men (or women). While they approve of the change, they hold this stance solely on account of their status as '**company figureheads**' who will never be caught up in the work of actually achieving it. Figureheads or yes-men have nothing of substance to add to the conversation, but seek merely to ingratiate themselves so that they are well-placed to share the benefits in the event of the project's success. If you are not careful, they could end up wasting a lot of your time.

- **Attitude**: Positive
- **Influence**: Low

3. The apparatchik

The apparatchik has much to say. Because apparatchiks achieved great success in the old world, they find it hard to imagine the new – and ever harder to imagine that the new actually works. **If a change story is to prevail, it is important that you bring the apparatchiks with you.** For one thing, they are motivated and thus valuable employees; for another, they are crucial to getting the gossipmongers on board.

- **Attitude**: Initially negative
- **Influence**: High

4. The guardian angel

Finally, there is the guardian angel. This is the optimal combination: plentiful influence and a positive attitude. It hardly need be said that representatives of this species are rare. **Guardian angels often need to be created**; for example, by winning over an apparatchik.

- **Attitude**: Positive
- **Influence**: High

A good story alone is not enough. If your change project is to succeed, you need the help of others; after all, even a superhero cannot save the world single-handedly. Before you can seek this help, you need to know which of your supposed allies are genuine and which could place your project in jeopardy.

3.2 How much do you know about the people you're talking to?

Knowing where to look for your stakeholders is only the beginning. Thus, it can be useful to create **a kind of 'character portrait'** of your key stakeholders in the same way a screenwriter or author would do. What do these people like? What are their hobbies? What metaphors and analogies can you use to inspire them? Such an approach will also quickly shed light on the things you *don't* know. Unfortunately, in my consulting work, I frequently observe how flippantly this subject is handled and how little managers actually know about those they are talking to – whether in change communication, sales or any other area.

Things to know about each of your stakeholders: Name, age, origin, social status, job title, education, marital status, religion, relationship, social milieu, favourite film/book, hobbies, values, temperament, motto for life, wishes and fears.

Why 'hobbies' and 'favourite film', you ask? Some time ago, I was involved in a project in which an established management consultancy (C1) was travelling very frequently to the premises of a particular client. Another consultancy, C2, was attempting to generate business with this client. The reason for the near-permanent presence of consultancy C1 on the client's premises was that the division manager was friends with a partner in the consultancy and, as such, was "hardly able to refuse." In an interesting twist, we were able to ascertain that this division manager was a big fan of mafia film *The Godfather*, and confronted him on his friendship with the partner using the famous Michael Corleone quote on the danger of mixing friendship and money ("Friendship and money – oil and water"). The division manager was delighted to have fans of *The Godfather* on the scene.

Of course, such insider knowledge cannot automatically turn a bad pitch into a good one, but **it *can* make the difference between getting the deal or missing the mark.**

Final checklist for stakeholders

Once you have ascertained what your stakeholders think, understood their influence and obtained some key information about them, try to answer the following. Ideally, you should be able to answer all nine questions.

Stakeholder checklist:

- ✓ Who is this person?
- ✓ What is their role?
- ✓ What is their attitude towards the project?
- ✓ What influence do they have?
- ✓ What motivates them on a personal level?
- ✓ What kind of relationship do you have to this person?
- ✓ Within the hierarchy, is this person
  - above you?
  - below you?
  - your equal?
- ✓ Which people outside the organization play a role in this person's decisions?
- ✓ What stories should you tell this person?

If you find yourself reading this and thinking, "That looks like hard work," you'd be right. However, it is many times harder to get a poorly-communicated, off-the-rails change initiative back on track. Make sure to invest **sufficient time in preparation**. As in so many other scenarios, the old Spartan saying "The more you sweat in training, the less you bleed in battle" is a good one to live by.

30 *Before you begin your change communication, you must consider the stakeholders to be addressed. By plotting them on two axes labelled 'power' and 'attitude', you can divide them into four meaningful groups. Pay particular attention to powerful people who are (initially) critical of the change.*

If you were writing a good thriller, you would need to think hard about the characters. With a change story, it's no different. The more you know about your stakeholders beyond job title and length of service, the better.

30 MINUTES

What do Beowulf, Frodo Baggins and Anakin Skywalker have to do with your change story?

Page 84

What true stories can you use to create desire for innovation?

Page 86

Why does the little shepherd boy David embody the start-up mentality?

Page 90

4. Explaining change clearly

As we all know, change projects are tricky because you are selling something new and thus not easily imaginable. You're not selling fancy shoes, watches or cars – nor are you selling iPhones, for which Apple fans used to camp out at the front of the shop so as not to miss new releases. When a consumer purchases such a product on impulse, their brain releases an instant shower of happiness hormones – a phenomenon known in neuromarketing as 'instant gratification'.

By contrast, your project bears an uninspiring title such as 'Digital Transformation', 'Global Shared Service Centre', 'Working Differently 4.0' or similar, with unwieldy terms that generate not fanciful images in the brain, but mistrust and resistance. **To explain complex processes in a brain-friendly way, you need pictures.** For this, you need example stories and metaphors.

4.1 Three tried-and-tested basic plots

Story experts say that there are approximately **seven basic plots**, some of which recur particularly frequently. Author Christopher Booker wrote about them in his book *The Seven Basic Plots*. We will look at three of these plots in this chapter.

Defeating the monster

In the Old English legend *Beowulf*, set in Scandinavia, the hero Beowulf fights a giant who is terrorizing a village. Beowulf injures the giant, follows the trail of blood and suddenly finds himself facing the giant's much more dangerous mother. The hit film *Jaws*, in which the hero is forced to go far out to sea to kill the shark, follows a similar sequence of events. *Alien*, in which the heroine Ripley takes on the alien single-handedly, transposes the same basic theme into space (and it is thus little surprise that "Jaws in space" is exactly how it was pitched). All of the above are classic stories of overcoming the monster. While it just so happens that the above examples involve literal monsters, it is important to note that this type of story can also play out **on a psychological level** (or on both levels at once). What is key is that the hero must stop something bad – just as the taxi driver Max had to stop the killer Vincent in *Collateral* or Clarice Starling had to stop the killer Buffalo Bill in *Silence of the Lambs*. A strategy story could be about stopping **a dangerous and increasingly powerful competitor**, perhaps by attacking them on their own turf.

The quest

Another basic plot is 'the quest', in which the hero is required to overcome numerous challenges before reaching the happy ending. This can be seen, for example, in *The Hobbit* or *Lord of the Rings*. The hero is often also required to deliver something, as with Frodo's mission to bring the Ring to Mount Doom or Vincent and Jules' delivery of the mysterious suitcase in *Pulp Fiction*. On a company level, such a plotline might be well suited **for communicating an international expansion involving various milestones and diversions.**

Rebirth

'Rebirth' is another common basic plot. Classic examples include the **transformation** of the biblical Saul to Paul, the transformation of the 'good' Anakin Skywalker to the evil Darth Vader (and back again), or Michael Corleone's reverse metamorphosis from law-abiding ex-marine to a mafia godfather. Fictional character Daniel LaRusso transforms himself multiple times in the *Karate Kid* films in the hopes of achieving a win, as does Rocky the boxer in the films of the same name. In a rebirth-themed strategy story, the **transformation might be a reimagining of the company as something entirely new** – a move pulled off very impressively by Axel Springer with its comprehensive digitalization strategy.

30 *Humans have been inventing stories for thousands of years. There are a certain number of 'story archetypes' whose basic sequences can be recognized in almost every story ever told. Such archetypes include 'defeating the monster', 'the quest' and 'rebirth'.*

4.2 Real-life stories as analogies for your strategy

Analogies work: indeed, the Bible states that even Jesus Christ recognized and used their power in the form of parables. Nowadays, however, companies avail themselves of this power far too infrequently. Back in chapter 1.2, we mentioned the half-hearted presentations given by managers to inform employees about 'Strategy 2020', 'Multichannel Germany' or 'Digital First'. The fact of the matter is that as long as these ideas remain abstract and lifeless, employees cannot begin to contemplate them. This is where real-life stories, aphorisms and analogies come in, since they help to make **abstract, not-yet-existing initiatives tangible.**

Example of innovation: ***Marconi and the radio waves***

In 1901, Guglielmo Marconi succeeded in his empirical experiment to transmit a Morse signal wirelessly from Europe to North America – the world's first radio transmission. It was with this signal transmission that the age of communication was officially ushered in. Yet according to the state of knowledge at the time, the experiment should never have succeeded. Physicists had repeatedly indicated that it would not be possible to transmit radio waves over more than 300 km because the curvature of the Earth's surface would cause them to drift into space. However, Marconi had made an interesting discovery: he had received radio signals from ships proven to be further than 300 km away. How could this be?

The explanation: The Earth's atmosphere contains a network of ions, the so-called 'ionosphere'. Radio waves are reflected off the ionosphere and bounced back down to Earth.

Marconi's success shows that it is less difficult to invent the new than to get rid of the 'old', i.e. to dispel existing beliefs.

Applicable to: Digital transformation, agile enterprise, innovation management.

Example of a successful takeover: ***The Norman conquest of England***

William the Conqueror conquered England at the Battle of Hastings in 1066. He won the battle with 'technological leadership' – with armoured knights, longbows and a better strategy. By any definition, it was a **'hostile takeover'.** However, it was afterwards that the real work began: William had to convince the Anglo-Saxon warlords to help him reposition England under the Norman flag. He did this by placing his trust in English noblemen to accomplish this process of integration in accordance with his wishes. Because of this pledge of confidence, few warlords took it upon themselves to betray or deceive William.

Great ventures can be steered by one of two methods: **control or trust.** William chose the latter. By opting to manage the **integration of the 'company'** (in this case, England) on a trust basis, he ensured that his post-merger integration was successful and had impacts lasting for thousands of years. The story also shows that **change management and post-merger integration (PMI)** are much more important than the type of merger being carried out. Everything that William the Conqueror brought to England as part of this hostile takeover eventually became a source of national pride for the Anglo-Saxons: the Tower of London, the system of nobility and knights and the House of Windsor, the most famous monarchy in the world.

Applicable to: Takeovers, PMI, change management.

Example of painful sacrifices: ***General Kutuzov and Napoleon***

Napoleon invaded Moscow in 1812. General Kutuzov, commander-in-chief of the Russian army at that time, made a rather surprising choice: he left Moscow with his troops so that Napoleon could take the city. In doing so, Kutuzov sacrificed Moscow, but saved Russia. Since Moscow had already run out of supplies, Napoleon's attack was fruitless and he was surprised by the harshness of the Russian winter, an event vividly described in Tolstoy's *War and Peace*. As Kutuzov later explained, if the army had not sacrificed Moscow, Napoleon would have taken all of Russia and Moscow with it. Paradoxically, by sacrificing Moscow, they not only saved Russia, but Moscow, too.

This story shows that it can be worthwhile to make painful sacrifices in aid of a greater good. Indeed, there are established companies that hold competitions for start-ups and reward the disruptive idea that is most likely to destroy the established business model. Often, it is necessary to part with an existing business model and attack and sacrifice the tools of one's past success to make way for future innovation.

Applicable to: Transformation, closure of business units, job cuts, cost-cutting.

Example of start-up thinking and agility: ***David and Goliath***

We all know the story of the little shepherd boy, David, who fought the giant Goliath. The special thing about this story is that David was a newcomer to the art of war: if he had known what he was getting into, he probably wouldn't have taken it on. Knowing nothing about war, David didn't choose a sword to fight with – as other warriors of King Saul would have done – but the only weapon he knew: the slingshot.

Interestingly, this was also the only weapon with which David could defeat Goliath from a safe distance.

David embodies the **attacker from the periphery** who, unlike the established companies ('incumbents'), does not yet know the market well enough to worry unduly. The story shows that success often lies in the **spirit of a beginner** – the one who dares to do new things – and that it can be beneficial for an innovation strategy to reflect on the **innovative spirit** of the early days. You might have heard the saying: "King Saul thought Goliath was too big to fight – David thought Goliath was too big to miss." This story also lends itself well to situations in which a small, agreeable company has to deal with a big, disagreeable competitor.

Applicable to: Innovation strategies, founder stories, expansion strategies, agility.

People have always told stories. Within the story-telling tradition, the same basic patterns crop up again and again. 30

Stories that make good examples or analogies can be found everywhere – in books, films and in your favourite series. Each time you come across a good story, ask whether it might be useful for a future change initiative. Become a story truffle pig!

You've read the book – now it's time for change

That brings us to the end of this little book, and I hope it has given you some insights into planning, explaining and anchoring change strategies in your company. It is important that you have the right people on board – at board level, management level and among your employees. Remember that managers, in particular, have an important role to play in implementing the strategy and that not everyone can or wishes to take on this role. You will sometimes need to be merciless. You cannot allow an entire change project (and with it, the future of the company) to be placed in jeopardy because a few nay-sayers are not pulling in the same direction. In this situation, even the best story cannot help. As unfortunate as it may sound, **change management can sometimes also mean changing the management.**

Fast Reader

1. Change is a necessary evil

Even if leadership coaches and retired managers are fond of propagating a rose-tinted picture, the truth is that we, as humans, are initially sceptical about any change. Those who fail to account for this in their change strategy will be doomed to fail from the off.

In order to plan change optimally, managers must consider the following:

- ***Strategy and change are natural bedfellows. A strategy is always the way to a goal. Any time you wish to do things differently and better than before, a strategy is essential.***
- ***The communication of change within a company is often sluggish and dull. This places the implementation of the change in jeopardy.***
- ***Innovations arise through change. Those who fail to drive innovation are driven by external forces.***

- ***Humans do not like the 'new' because it puts our brain on alert for danger. Managers must take employees' fears seriously.***

2. The change story

It is often not clear to employees why a change is necessary at all. What makes the difference here is a good change story.

30 ***If you wish to anchor your change story in the company, you must consider the following:***

- ***Every hero needs a villain and every solution a problem. It must be clear that the change is worth the effort and what will become better as a result.***
- ***Even if you fail to tell a story, this doesn't mean that no story will be told. In the worst case scenario, gossip and rumours will spring up to fill the gap.***
- ***Every good change story must follow the 'four-note chord': situation, disaster, turning point and happy ending.***

3. Allies for your change project

For all their careful strategy planning, managers often make the mistake of forgetting who they are talking to. Those who do not succeed in persuading the relevant stakeholders will be unable to implement their strategies.

Good stakeholder management means:

- ***You need to know what degree of influence*** 30
each person has in the organization and how they are disposed towards the change.
- ***Just as a screenplay needs character descriptions, you need a certain amount of information about each of the people you are talking to. If you do not understand what makes them tick, getting them on-side will be almost impossible.***

4. Explaining change clearly

The Bible tells us that Jesus Christ used parables to represent difficult ideas as simple images. By the same token, managers who use the power of analogy to portray change in a vivid and tangible way give their strategy the best chance of being understood by the listeners' brains.

30 ***Tried-and-tested basic plots and real-life examples can help to bring complex processes to life.***

- ***Like a good film, an effective change story follows a clear pattern of dramatic events. Typical basic plots include, for example, 'defeating the monster', 'quest' or 'rebirth'.***
- ***Examples and analogies can illustrate facts that would otherwise be difficult to grasp. For example, the story of David and Goliath can stand for start-up thinking, William the Conqueror for optimal change management or General Kutuzov for the necessity of doing away with an old business model and adopting a new one.***

About the author

Prof. Dr. Veit Etzold is Germany's number one speaker and consultant for strategy communication and storytelling. After a career in strategy consulting (BCG) and a number of other fields, he now advises a number of DAX corporations, medium-sized enterprises, banks, consultancies, and start-ups. With ten *Spiegel* bestsellers, Prof. Etzold is also one of the most successful thriller authors in Germany. He holds a doctorate in media sciences and an MBA from the IESE Business School. In addition, he teaches marketing, sales, strategic management and storytelling at the Aalen University of Applied Sciences in Baden-Württemberg, where he also heads the Competence Centre for Neuromarketing.
His podcast 'To Tell is to Sell – als Führungskraft endlich richtig verstanden werden' ['To Tell is to Sell – How to finally be understood as a manager'] was one of the ten most successful business podcasts on iTunes on its launch. Also published by GABAL is Prof. Etzold's previous (German-language) guide to strategy, entitled *Strategie: Planen, erklären, umsetzen [Strategy: Plan, explain, implement]*.

The author can be reached at **info@veit-etzold.com**, at **www.veit-etzold.com** and on +49 030/39 74 36 67.

Further reading

- Bargh, John A: *The Unconscious Mind.* New Haven: Yale University, 2008
- Booker, Christopher: *The Seven Basic Plots.* New York: Bloomsburg, 2016
- Drucker, Peter: *Management.* New York: Harper Collins, 2008
- Etzold, Veit: *Strategie: Planen, erklären, umsetzen.* Offenbach: GABAL, 2018
- Etzold, Veit: *Der weiße Hai im Weltraum – Storytelling für Manager.* Weinheim: Wiley, 2016 (2. Auflage)
- Etzold, Veit: 'Was überzeugt den Kunden?'. *Harvard Business Manager.* Hamburg: Spiegel Verlag, October 2013
- Etzold, Veit: 'Richtig Präsentieren'. *Harvard Business Manager.* Hamburg: Spiegel Verlag, März 2019
- Fitzsimons, Gráinne; Chartrand, Tanya; Fitzsimons, Gavan: 'Automatic Effects of Brand Exposure on Motivated Behavior: How Apple Makes You "Think Different"', *Journal of Consumer Research,* Vol. 35, June 2008, p. 21–35
- Gladwell, Malcolm: *The Tipping Point.* New York: Backbay Books, 2008
- Gombrich, E. H.: *Kunst und Illusion.* Berlin: Phaidon, 2002
- Henderson, Bruce: 'Das Konzept der Strategie', in: Oetinger, Bolko von (ed.): *Das Boston Consulting Group Strategie-Buch,* Munich: Econ, 2000, p. 54 ff.

- Kahneman, Daniel; Kentsch, Jack; Thaler, Richard: 'Experimental Tests of the Endowment Effect and the Coase Theorem,' in: *Journal of Political Economy*, Vol. 98. Chicago: The University of Chicago Press, 1990, p. 1325–1348
- Kahneman, Daniel: *Schnelles Denken, langsames Denken*. Munich: Penguin Verlag, 2012
- Kaplan, Robert S.; Norton, David P.: *The Strategy-Focused Organization*. Boston: Harvard Business Review, 1998
- Kotter, John: *Leading Change*. Munich: Vahlen, 2011
- Lafley, A. G.; Martin, Roger, et al.: 'Die Kunst der Strategieplanung', in: 'Strategie'. Hamburg: *Harvard Business Manager*, Edition, 1/2019
- Machiavelli, Niccolò: *Il Principe/Der Fürst*. Stuttgart: Reclam, 2000
- Scheier, Christian; Held, Dirk: 'Die Neuro-Logik erfolgreicher Markenkommunikation', in: Häusel, Hans-Georg (ed.): *Neuromarketing*. Munich: Haufe, 2014, p. 78 ff.
- Senge, P. M.: *The Fifth Discipline*. New York: Currency, 1990
- Sull, Donald; Homkes, Rebecca; Sull, Charles: 'Von der Strategie zur Umsetzung', in: 'Strategie'. Hamburg: *Harvard Business Manager*, Edition, 1/2019
- Sunzi: *Die Kunst des Krieges*. Munich: Knaur, 1998
- Thiel, Peter: *Zero to One: Notes on Startups or how to build the future*. London: Virgin Books, 2014

- Wood, Wendy; Neal, David: 'The habitual consumer', in: *Journal of Consumer Psychology*. New York: Wiley, 2009

Websites:

- www.hassonlab.com, last accessed 14.01.2021
- https://hbr.org/2009/02/tropicanas-marketing-folly.html, last accessed 14.01.2021
- https://www.youtube.com/watch?v=Ug83sF_3_Ec&t=60s, last accessed 14.01.2021
- http://www.dhmo.de/fakten.html, last accessed 14.01.2021

Interviews:

- Interview with Prof. Dr. Gerhard Roth by author at the Hanse Wissenschaftskolleg Institute of Advanced Study, Delmenhorst, October 2004

Index

Testimonials

"Change and transformation are challenges that all our customers face. Veit Etzold is a master of using storytelling not only to plan strategies, but to ensure that all employees are brought on board."
Gerd Kulhavy, Chairman of the Board, Speakers Excellence

"The financial industry is among the most profoundly changed by digital transformation. Veit Etzold shows how new strategies and change projects can be executed successfully without bringing an organisation to a standstill. A must for every business practitioner."
Marcus Vitt, Spokesman of the Board of Management, DONNER & REUSCHEL AG

"It's remarkable how Veit Etzold succeeds in weaving complex subject matter and 'marketing talk' into inspiring stories."
Uschi Durant, Head of Joint TV Marketing Screenforce, Mediengruppe RTL Deutschland GmbH

"The archives are brimming with brilliant yet ultimately unrealised strategies – mostly because the need for and purpose of the strategy was not anchored clearly enough within the organisation. The emotionally targeted, sustained communication of a strategy is the first step to successful implementation. Veit Etzold shows the right way to do it."
Dr. Peter Strüven, Economic and Political Consultant, Former Chairman of Germany and Asia, The Boston Consulting Group (BCG)

"No matter how ingenious the business idea, how innovative the product or how revolutionary the service – without the right marketing strategy, conquering the market will remain an elusive goal. Customers do not merely want to be reached and communicated with, but genuinely inspired. Veit Etzold gets right to the heart of what matters."
Wolfgang Bosbach, Lawyer, Long-time Expert on Interior Policy at the German Federal Parliament